FOOTSTEPS

THE
Romans

Sally Hewitt

Contents

3000 BC — 2000 BC — 1000 BC — 0 — 1000 AD — 2000 AD

Egyptians

Greeks

Romans

Vikings

W

FRANKLIN WATTS

NEW YORK • LONDON • SYDNEY

Who were the Romans?

The Romans came from the ancient city of Rome. Legends tell how twin brothers, Romulus and Remus, were thrown into the River Tiber by their uncle. A wolf rescued them and took care of them. When they grew up they built the city of Rome, and Romulus became its first king.

The Romans became very powerful and conquered the countries surrounding them. The ruler of the whole Roman Empire was called the Emperor.

The people of the Roman Empire were divided into three groups. Roman citizens could vote in elections and serve in the army. Non-citizens could not vote. Slaves had no freedom and were owned by citizens.

3

Roman sandals

Romans wore leather boots tied with thongs.
When they were indoors they wore simple sandals.

You will need:

Cardboard   Hole puncher   Scissors
Two long pieces of string, or very long shoelaces

Follow the steps . . .

1. Stand on the cardboard and draw around both of your feet. Cut out the shapes you have drawn.

2. Punch holes round the edges of the foot shapes.

3. Sit down and put your feet on the sandals. One at a time, thread the laces through the holes and over your feet.

Jewellery

Many Romans believed that if they wore a
snake bracelet they would lead a long life.

You will need:

| White paper | Thin cardboard | Glue |
| Gold paint | Scissors | Pencil |

Follow the steps . . .

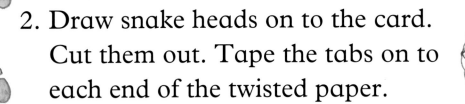

1. Twist a long rectangle of white
   paper round and round.
   Cut it to fit round your wrist.

2. Draw snake heads on to the card.
   Cut them out. Tape the tabs on to
   each end of the twisted paper.

3. Paint the bracelets with gold paint
   and let them dry. Make or paint eyes.

4. You could try making brooches too.

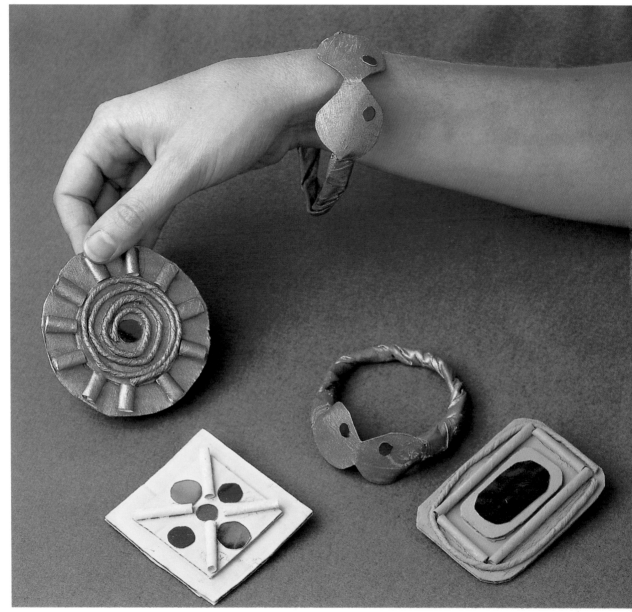

Life in a Roman town

Walls were built around Roman towns to keep them safe from attack. Two main roads entered the gates and crossed the town from north to south and from east to west.

The busy market place in the centre was surrounded by shops and public buildings. People packed into the theatre and amphitheatre for entertainment, and visited the public baths. They built temples to the gods.

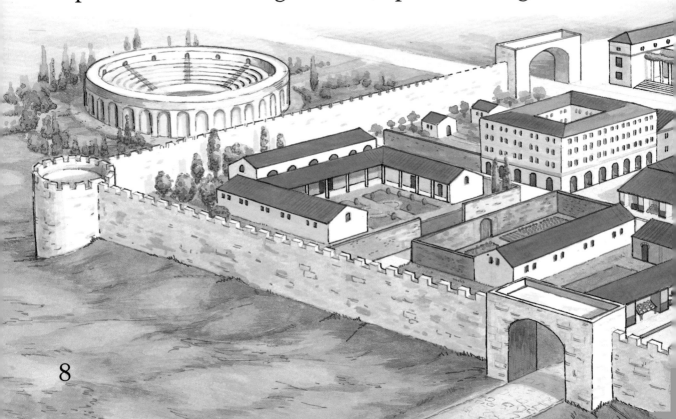

A *domus* was a private house owned by rich people. It had many rooms set round an open courtyard. Slaves did all the housework.

Insulae were apartment blocks up to five stories high. Water was fetched from fountains and waste was thrown out of the windows. There were no kitchens, so people bought hot meals in snack bars.

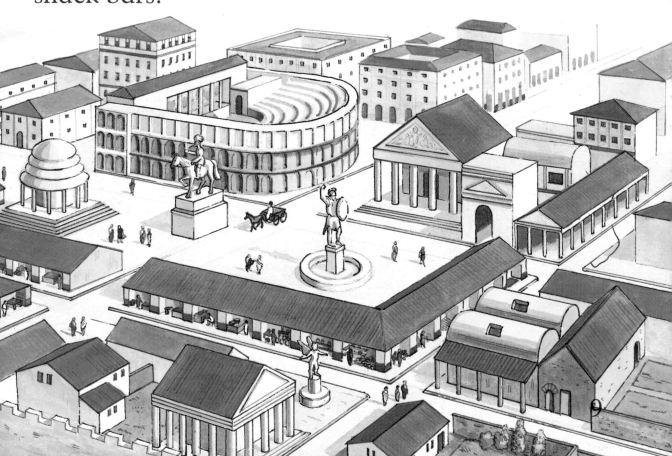

Mosaic picture

Wealthy people decorated their floors with mosaic pictures. They were made using tiny pieces of coloured stone.

You will need:

Cardboard   Coloured paper   Pencil
Scissors   Glue

Follow the steps . . .

1. Draw the outline of a picture on to the cardboard.

2. Draw a simple pattern round the edge.

3. Cut the coloured paper into small pieces.

4. Glue the pieces on to your pencil outline to make a colourful mosaic.

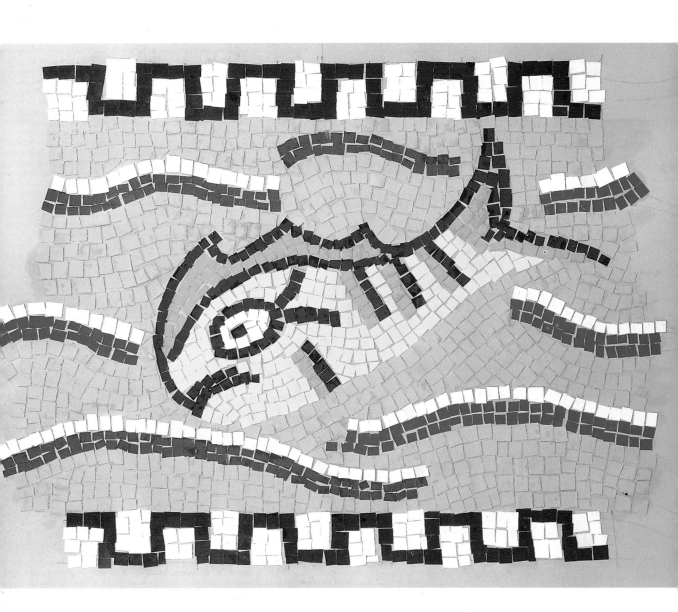

The Roman army

The strength of the mighty Roman Empire depended on its army. The Roman army conquered new lands, protected the Empire against its enemies and kept the peace.

Roman soldiers had to walk to all corners of the Empire. As they went, they built thousands of kilometres of roads.

Soldiers trained hard every day. Three times a month they practised marching 30 kilometres at a very fast pace. They wore their armour as they marched. They carried their shield, weapons, leg-protectors and a heavy pack of tools and food.

Life was tough for soldiers, but they were paid well. When they retired they were given money or a small plot of land.

13

A Roman soldier

A foot soldier wore a helmet, a metal vest, an apron of metal-studded straps, and strong sandals.

You will need:

Cardboard

Silver foil

Pencil

Red crepe paper

Brown paper

Paint

Scissors

Glue

Follow the steps . . .

1. Paint the outline of a soldier on to the cardboard. Cut these shapes for the helmet.

2. Cut strips of:
   – red paper for the tunic
   – foil for the vest
   – brown paper for the apron
   Make balls of foil for the apron.

3. Glue everything on to your soldier outline.

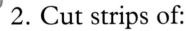

A Roman standard

A group of eighty soldiers was called a century.

Each century had an emblem called a standard.

You will need:

Cardboard	2 cardboard tubes	PVA glue
Red crepe paper	Scissors	Pencil
Sticky tape	Silver foil	Paints

Follow the steps . . .

1. Copy these shapes on to the cardboard. Cut them out. Paint the sun yellow.

2. Wrap the other shapes in foil. Press them flat. Tape the cardboard tubes together.

3. Cut strips of card. Stick the foil shapes onto the strips. Glue them to the tube.

4. Glue crepe paper ribbons on to the rectangle. Add a red fringe to the semi-circle.

A shield and sword

Soldiers could hold their shields together like this to make a protective shell.

You will need:

Cardboard box   Gold cardboard   Glue
Sticky tape   Scissors   Paints
Paintbrush

Follow the steps . . .

1. Cut out the base of the box and paint it red.

2. Cut a rectangle and arrows out of gold cardboard. Glue them on your shield. Decorate the edges.

3. Make a boss from a circle of gold cardboard. Glue it on the centre of the shield.

4. Make a handle with the sides of the box. Tape it to the back of the shield. Cut out a sword too.

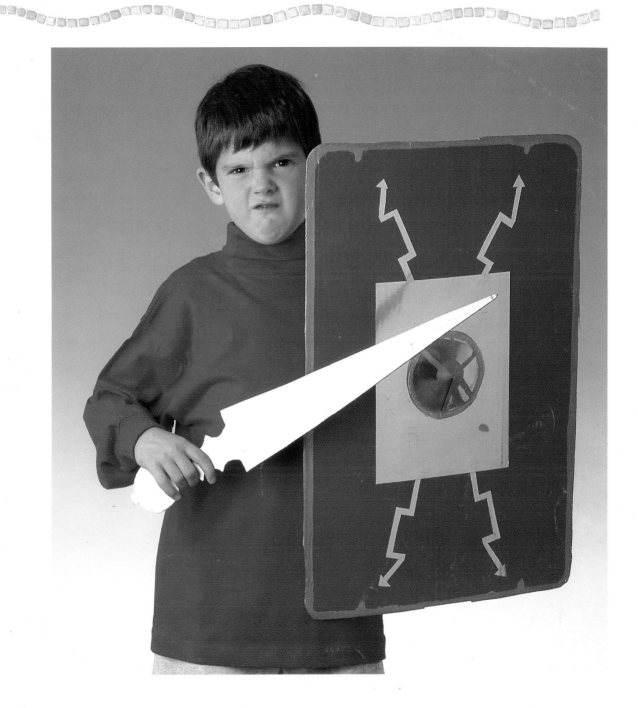

A visit to the baths

Roman people enjoyed going to the baths. It was a place to meet friends, play games and relax. Men and women went at different times. Children were allowed in free.

Visitors left their clothes in a cloakroom and went for a cold dip in the *frigidarium*. Next they went into the *tepidarium* for a warm dip.

After that they went into the hot and steamy
caldarium. It made them sweat. When they
came out, olive oil was rubbed into their skin
and scraped off with a *strigil.* Finally they
jumped into the cold pool to cool off.

The baths were heated by large fires under
the floor.

Roman numerals

You can write Roman numerals using only these seven letters:

I	V	X	L	C	D	M
1	5	10	50	100	500	1000

You will need:

Pencil   Paper

Follow the steps . . .

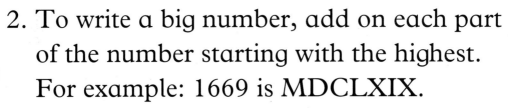

1. Practise writing Roman numerals.

2. To write a big number, add on each part of the number starting with the highest. For example: 1669 is MDCLXIX.
   M (1000), DC (500+100), LX (50+10), IX (9).

3. Read the date in the photograph opposite. The answer is upside down at the bottom.

4. Can you write the year you were born?

To count from 1 to 20 in Roman numerals, add or subtract letters like this:

I	II	III	IV	V	VI	VII	VIII	IX	X
1	1+1	1+1+1	5-1	5	5+1	5+1+1	5+1+1+1	10-1	10

XI	XII	XIII	XIV	XV	XVI	XVII	XVIII	XIX	XX
10+1	10+1+1	10+1+1+1	10+(5-1)	10+5	10+5+1	10+5+1+1	10+5+1+1+1	10+(10-1)	10+10

Count by tens like this

X	XX	XXX	XL	L	LX	LXX	LXXX	XC	C
10	10+10	10+10+10	50-10	50	50+10	50+10+10	50+10+10+10	100-10	100

1976

INDEX

Entries in *italics* are activity pages.

© 1995 Franklin Watts
This edition 1998

Franklin Watts
96 Leonard Street
London EC2A 4RH

Franklin Watts Australia
14 Mars Road
Lane Cove
NSW 2066

UK ISBN 0 7496 1875 2

Dewey Decimal Classification 937

Editor: Annabel Martin
Consultant: Richard Tames
Design: Mike Davis
Artwork: Cilla Eurich
 Ruth Levy
Photography: Peter Millard

A CIP catalogue record for this book is available from the British Library.

Printed in Malaysia